Findings and Recommendations on California's Permanent Partial Disability System

Executive Summary

Rachel Kaganoff Stern

Mark A. Peterson

Robert T. Reville

Mary E. Vaiana

RAND

The Institute for Civil Justice

THE INSTITUTE FOR CIVIL JUSTICE

The mission of the Institute for Civil Justice is to help make the civil justice system more efficient and more equitable by supplying policymakers and the public with the results of objective, empirically based, analytic research. The ICJ facilitates change in the civil justice system by analyzing trends and outcomes, identifying and evaluating policy options, and bringing together representatives of different interests to debate alternative solutions to policy problems. The Institute builds on a long tradition of RAND research characterized by an interdisciplinary, empirical approach to public policy issues and rigorous standards of quality, objectivity, and independence.

ICJ research is supported by pooled grants from corporations, trade and professional associations, and individuals; by government grants and contracts; and by private foundations. The Institute disseminates its work widely to the legal, business, and research communities, and to the general public. In accordance with RAND policy, all Institute research products are subject to peer review before publication. ICJ publications do not necessarily reflect the opinions or policies of the research sponsors or of the ICJ Board of Overseers.

BOARD OF OVERSEERS

PREFACE

This volume summarizes a comprehensive empirical analysis of the permanent partial disability component of California's workers' compensation system. Established early in this century, this system processes hundreds of thousands of claims from injured workers every year and pays out billions of dollars in benefits. It has been widely criticized as complicated and providing minimal compensation at high costs.

Reform legislation in 1993 established the Commission on Health and Safety and Workers' Compensation, a politically balanced body meant to oversee and deal with possible changes in the system. One of the commission's charges was to evaluate the system's permanent partial disability component. The evaluation was conducted by RAND's Institute for Civil Justice.

The results of this evaluation should be of interest to a wide variety of participants in California's workers' compensation system, including employers, insurers, attorneys, and employee groups. The study findings will also be useful to workers' compensation experts in other states that are considering changes in their workers' compensation systems.

In light of these diverse audiences, we present our findings in several forms. This volume summarizes our methods and findings. A detailed discussion of the evaluation can be found in *Compensating Permanent Workplace Injuries: A Study of the California System*, Mark A. Peterson, Robert T. Reville, and Rachel Kaganoff Stern, with Peter S. Barth, MR-920-ICJ, 1997.

The study was a collaborative effort. Mark A. Peterson led the research. Robert T. Reville was responsible for the wage loss analysis. Rachel Kaganoff Stern led the qualitative analysis of the workers' compensation process. Peter S. Barth conducted the multi-state comparison.

For more information about the Institute for Civil Justice, contact:

Dr. Deborah R. Hensler, Director
Institute for Civil Justice
RAND
1700 Main Street
Santa Monica, CA 90407-2138
TEL: (310) 451-6916
FAX: (310) 451-6979
Internet: Deborah_Hensler@rand.org

A profile of the ICJ, abstracts of its publications, and ordering information can be found on RAND's home page on the World Wide Web at http://www.rand.org/centers/icj.

CONTENTS

FIGURES

ACKNOWLEDGMENTS

We would like to extend our sincere thanks to Christine Baker, the Executive Director of the Commission on Health and Safety and Workers' Compensation, for her expert guidance and support throughout this research project. We are also grateful to the members of the Commission on Health and Safety and Workers' Compensation and the advisory group on workers' compensation, many of whom spent considerable time responding to our questions and providing research advice and direction.

The Workers' Compensation Insurance Rating Bureau (WCIRB) and several California state agencies assisted us by providing us with data and helping us to understand the databases. Dave Bellusci at the WCIRB was enormously helpful, as were Michele Bunds and Rich Kihlthau at the State of California Employment Development Department (EDD). We also thank Blair Megowan and Del Gaines at the Disability Evaluation Unit; Ted Sorich, Jim Culbeaux, Russ Roeckel and Elizabeth Nisperos at the Department of Industrial Relations Data Processing; Walt Gladwin at the WCIRB; and Dave Jones at the EDD. We are grateful to the many members of the broader workers' compensation community who agreed to participate in our qualitative interviews.

John Burton at Rutgers and Bob Schoeni at RAND reviewed our report and their suggestions improved it immeasurably. Sue Polich prepared the complex data files for analysis and provided invaluable assistance throughout the study.

Finally, we thank Frank Neuhauser at Berkeley and our RAND colleagues Lloyd Dixon, Deborah Hensler, Dan McCaffrey, Erik Moller, and Pat Williams for their contributions to the project. Any errors that remain are our responsibility.

1. INTRODUCTION

California's workers' compensation system embodies a historic bargain struck early in this century between labor and employers. Workers injured on the job gave up the right to sue their employers for full but uncertain damages under tort liability in exchange for limited but certain benefits under a statutory compensation system. In return, workers receive medical treatment, temporary disability payments until they return to work, rehabilitation benefits (added in 1975), and financial compensation for their permanent disabilities. Permanent benefits are based on workers' disabilities, defined by statute as the loss of capacity to compete in the open labor market.

California's workers' compensation system is large, complex, and litigious.

California's system is vast. There are more than 300,000 claims annually in the state; billions of dollars are paid in benefits. In recent years, employers' tab for insurance premiums ran between $6 billion and $9 billion a year. This total excludes the costs for firms self-insuring their workers, who account for approximately 30 percent of the losses in the state.

The system has been widely criticized. It is procedurally complicated. It provides minimal compensation at high costs. System participants believe that ratings are often inconsistent, benefits unpredictable, and the validity of ratings questionable. Many stakeholders complain that the system is too litigious.

Major statutory changes in 1989 and 1993 attempted to address some of these concerns. The 1993 reform legislation established the Commission on Health and Safety and Workers' Compensation, a politically balanced body meant to oversee and deal with possible changes in the system. One of the commission's charges was to evaluate the system for determining payment for permanent partial disability (PPD). This executive summary provides the highlights of that evaluation, conducted by RAND's Institute for Civil Justice (ICJ).

The ICJ was asked by the Commission on Health and Safety and Workers' Compensation to evaluate California's PPD system.

The ICJ's evaluation was based on six related tasks:

- Detailed qualitative interviews with more than 50 key participants in two matched sets of interviews in Northern and Southern California;

- A review of the pertinent literature;

- A review of important recent developments in the treatment of PPD claims in other states;

- "Stakeholder" interviews with representatives of principal interest groups who operate in or are affected by the workers' compensation system;

- Statistical analyses of major databases describing the processing of workers' compensation claims;

- A wage loss study that examined the financial effects of permanent disabilities on injured workers and the validity of the current disability rating system.

2. THE HISTORY OF WORKERS' COMPENSATION IN CALIFORNIA

Workers' compensation programs were an outcome of the Progressive Era, when reformers responded to both labor and employer concerns about high rates of work-related injuries, insufficient compensation to injured workers, and continuing employer uncertainty about how to predict the costs related to these injuries. California's workers' compensation system was established in 1913 by the Boynton Act, which required that employers, with some exceptions such as the agricultural sector, provide workers' compensation benefits to their employees. Benefits for permanent disability, including permanent partial disability, were an essential part of the workers' compensation scheme.

In California, injured workers who have suffered some level of permanent disability begin to receive PPD benefits when (a) they have returned to work after an injury or (b) their condition is judged unlikely to improve further, even with additional medical treatment. PPD payments are meant to compensate workers for their disability, specifically for their lost ability to compete in the open labor market.

Permanent disability is intended to compensate for a worker's lost ability to compete in the labor market.

There are several reasons why California measures disability by this abstraction—lost ability to compete—rather than by simply looking at how much income a worker has lost. First, income loss frequently continues past the date when benefits are determined so that the total income loss cannot simply be added up. Second, workers' incentives to return to work could be weakened if their benefits were directly determined by the amount of income they lost. Third, determining benefits directly from lost income would poorly reward workers who show the most initiative in returning to work and would over-reward those who make the least effort.

Disability ratings are determined by a disability schedule that assesses the effect of scheduled injuries among workers in different occupations and adjusts for age. The higher the rating, the larger the number of weeks of benefits the worker receives, from 3 weeks for the lowest ratings to 694 weeks followed by lower-value life annuities for the highest. Permanent partial disability payments are based on the disability rating as well as on pre-injury wages; they have a ceiling of $230 per week for the highest disability ratings and $140 per week for the lowest.

The rating schedule includes virtually every form of disability, and ratings based on the schedule are deemed *prima facie* evidence of disability in any compensation proceeding. In practice, however, and for a variety of reasons, schedule-based computations of disability level can be the source of many disputes.

The PPD rating is the source of many disputes.

- Subjective medical findings such as pain enter into the calculation of disability ratings.

- Every factor determining disability ratings can be disputed in some circumstance.

- The primacy of medical reports as the basis for awarding PPD benefits may transform the adjudication process into a contest between competing medical evaluations.

Litigation may be exacerbated by a statutory provision that entitles an employee to reimbursement for medical-legal expenses necessarily incurred in making a claim, even if the claim is later deemed non-compensable. Expenses can include costs for x-rays, laboratory fees, diagnostic tests, medical records, medical reports, medical testimony, and legal fees necessary to prove a contested claim.

Major reforms of the workers' compensation system were implemented in 1989 and 1993; their full effects are yet unknown.

In 1989 and 1993, California implemented major statutory changes to address a broad range of workers' compensation issues. Highlights of these reforms include restructuring the medical-legal process, limiting compensability of psychiatric and post-termination claims, increasing benefit payments for moderate and serious disabilities, capping vocational rehabilitation payments, increasing fraud deterrence, and deregulating insurance rates.

It is still too early to assess the full effects of these reforms. Cases operating under the pre-1989 rules are still in the system; some that are subject to the 1989 rules, rather than the newer 1993 rules, are still open. But our interviews with system participants, described below, give some sense of how the reforms have affected the functioning and outcomes of the PPD system.

3. QUALITATIVE PORTRAIT OF THE WORKERS' COMPENSATION SYSTEM

Our interviews with knowledgeable participants in the workers' compensation system provided insight into how the system really operates, helped us take account of the diverse concerns of system participants, and gave us a sense of how participants felt the system had been affected by the 1989 and 1993 reforms. These limited interviews did not themselves drive our conclusions about California's PPD system; however, they helped direct our quantitative analyses, which were free of the inherent unrepresentativeness and self-interested biases of the interview materials.

We interviewed a broad variety of system participants in two matched sets—in the north and in the south of the state. They included applicant and defense attorneys, treating physicians, forensic physicians (experts who specialize in providing workers' compensation evaluations), third-party claims administrators, self-insured firms, insurers, and staff of the Division of Workers' Compensation, including representatives of the Disability Evaluation Unit (DEU), the Workers' Compensation Appeals Board (WCAB), and the Industrial Medical Council—entities responsible for evaluating or processing workers' compensation claims.

Our interviews and review of prior quantitative analyses indicated that the 1989 and 1993 reforms brought about the following changes: The number of PPD claims, workers' compensation premiums, and insurer's costs have decreased; medical costs have fallen sharply; and abusive claims practices have been reduced. Views about whether specific changes improved the workers' compensation system were mixed. However, everyone we interviewed agreed that the system remains highly adversarial and litigious, that it is excessively complex—now even more so as a result of the legislative changes, that the system is increasingly impenetrable to persons who are not regulars, and that it is a costly system delivering modest benefits.

Interviews suggest that reforms in 1989 and 1993 generally improved the system, but serious problems linger.

There was a general feeling across participant groups that despite reductions in the number of claims filed, the system is still overwhelmed. Many members of the insurance, employer, and attorney communities complained about continuing delays in claims processing and evaluation at the Disability Evaluation Unit and at the Workers' Compensation Appeals Board. In addition, increased system complexity has caused insurers, third-party administrators, and attorneys to substantially reduce the caseload that they can expect adjusters and attorneys to manage.

Many participants feel the system remains overwhelmed with claims.

Many physicians are not well prepared to evaluate industrial injuries.

There was concern, but little agreement, about how to improve the quality of medical evaluations used as the basis for determining ratings. Insurers, employers, attorneys, and even physicians themselves admitted that many doctors submitting medical evaluations are not well prepared for this important task. Many who expressed such concern also wanted to eliminate the current "presumption of correctness" afforded to treating physicians—that is, the heavy reliance upon the disability rating derived from evaluations by treating physicians.

Views of the disability rating process diverge sharply.

Both participant and stakeholder interviews revealed sharply divergent views about key features of the treatment of PPD claims, particularly the process for determining disability ratings. Employers, insurers, and some defense lawyers complained that the disability schedule, particularly its reliance on unverifiable subjective findings, produced inconsistent ratings and unnecessary litigation. On the other hand, applicant lawyers and some defense lawyers found the disability schedule and process workable, with the flexibility needed to address fairly the enormous variety of PPD claims.

4. WAGE LOSS STUDY

Our wage loss study is central to evaluating the treatment of PPD claims. California law states that the amount of PPD benefits should reflect injured workers' reduced ability to compete in an open labor market, a competitive disadvantage that should be reflected in a reduction of post-injury income derived from wages. The amount of this *wage loss* provides a potential empirical measure of disability: the larger the percentage of wages that a worker loses after injury, the larger the disability. Analyses of wage loss also provide an empirical measure of the adequacy of workers' compensation benefits—that is, the fraction of a worker's wage loss that is replaced by such benefits.

One measure of the adequacy of workers' compensation benefits is the fraction of wage loss replaced.

To investigate these issues, we obtained California Employment Development Department (EDD) data on quarterly earnings between 1989 and 1996 for 30,000 PPD applicants who had workplace injuries between 1991 and 1994. These data provided several years of information about each worker's earnings both before and after the injury. We then linked the EDD wage data for each worker to Workers' Compensation Insurance Rating Bureau (WCIRB) data on disability ratings, date of injury, and benefits paid.

The wage loss analysis requires comparing an observable number—workers' actual post-injury wages, which we obtained from the EDD—with an unobservable, hypothetical number—what workers would have earned, but for their injuries. To estimate the latter, we obtained actual EDD wages for a matched control group, i.e., uninjured workers who were working in the same firm at the same time and for similar wages as the PPD claimants to whom they were matched.

By comparing wages of injured and control workers before the injury date, we were able to support the reasonableness of using the controls' post-injury wages as an estimate of what injured workers would have earned, but for their injuries. Average wages for PPD claimants and control workers were virtually identical as far back as our data went, up to five years before the injury.

Injured workers' wage losses can occur in two different ways. First, the injury may remove a worker from the labor market (either temporarily or permanently) so that the worker has no earnings. Second, when working, the worker may earn less than he/she otherwise would have. The wage loss comparisons showed that injured workers suffered both types of losses and that, in combination, the loss was profound.

PPD claimants experience significant time out of work, compared to similar uninjured workers.

Workplace injuries are followed by long and often recurrent reductions in time at work; these absences cause significant wage losses.

Figure 1 shows the ratio of the number of injured workers at work to the number of control workers at work over the period before and after the former's injury. The ratio is reported by the disability rating of the injured worker. Beginning with the quarter in which the injury occurs, injured workers experience significant reductions in time at work, and the reductions increase with the disability rating. Even four and five years *after* the injury, injured workers continue to experience more time out of work than their controls. The difference at five years ranges from 10 percent fewer working among the lowest disability rating to more than 50 percent fewer working at the highest rating.

Even after five years, PPD claimants who have returned to work earn 20 percent less than comparable uninjured workers.

When PPD claimants return to work after their injuries, they receive substantially lower wages. Figure 2 shows before-tax quarterly wages among the PPD claimants compared to wages for controls who are working. The gap between the two sets of wages represents PPD claimants' wage losses as measured by the difference between the groups' quarterly income from wages while both worked. This pattern of reduced income from wages for injured workers continues throughout the four to five years of data covered by our analyses.

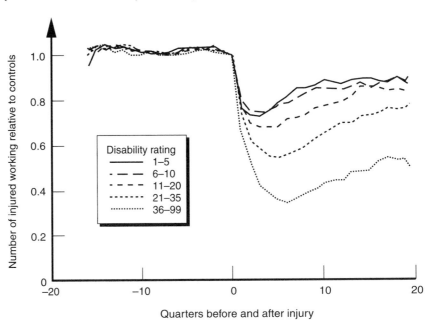

Figure 1—Ratio of Number of Workers Injured Between 1991 and 1993
Working in Quarter to Number of Matched Controls Working,
by Disability Rating

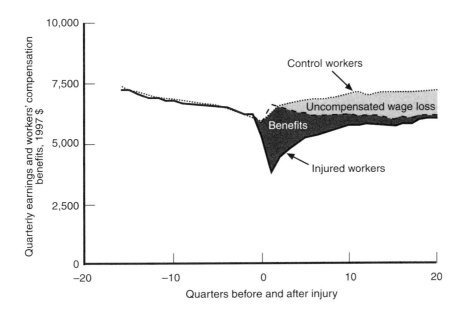

Figure 2—Mean Quarterly Wages and Benefits for Injured Workers Injured Between 1991 and 1993 and Controls, Including Only Quarters When Both Are Working

Figure 3 compares average quarterly before-tax earnings of the injured workers and controls, including zero income for either controls or injured workers not at work. Together the shaded areas represent the full measure of earnings loss from both reduced wages and increased time out of work.

The combined effect of reduced wages and increased time out of work is profound.

The joint effect of both losses is profound: Injured workers spend less time at work and, when working, earn less than their controls. For example, PPD claimants injured in 1991 and 1992 received approximately 40 percent less earnings than their controls over the four to five years after their injuries.

A primary objective of California's workers' compensation system is to ameliorate injury-related wage losses and support workers for some period of time until they can adjust to their changed financial circumstances. The system provides temporary disability benefits during the initial period after an injury, maintenance for workers in vocational rehabilitation programs, and permanent partial disability benefits after workers return to work or when their medical conditions stabilize. The goal of temporary benefits is to replace two-thirds of the pre-injury wage. The goal of permanent benefits is to compensate for lost ability to compete. We measure this lost ability as wages lost and assume that the goal for permanent partial disability compensation is comparable to the goal for temporary benefits: the replacement of two-thirds of wages lost.

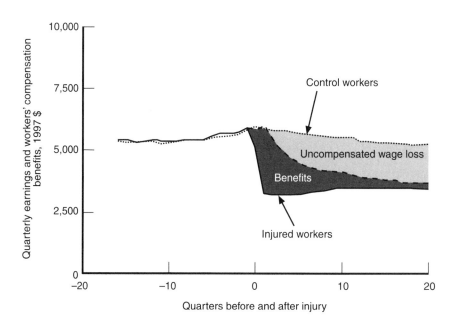

Figure 3—Mean Quarterly Wages and Benefits for Injured Workers Injured Between 1991 and 1993 and Controls, Including Injury-Related Time Out of Work

Total benefits compensate 40 to 50 percent of wage loss.

Figures 2 and 3 illustrate how much of the wage loss (i.e., the gap between PPD claimants' wages and controls' wages) is reduced by workers' compensation benefits and how much remains uncompensated. The benefits counted include temporary disability, permanent partial disability, and vocational rehabilitation maintenance allowance. For represented claimants, benefits also include the fees paid to lawyers. During the first five years the benefits failed to meet the objective of compensating injured workers for two-thirds of wage loss. Benefits totaled slightly less than 40 percent of workers' full losses—losses both from being out of work and from their reduced wages during employment (Figure 3). Even using the conservative estimate of wage loss shown on Figure 2 (wages lost during the initial period of employment after injury and then differences in wages between PPD claimants and controls when both were working), benefits compensated slightly less than half of wage loss.

We simulated three adjustments to our analyses to investigate the sensitivity of our results to various limitations of our data.

- We examined how taxes affect wage replacement. Benefits are tax free and therefore more valuable than the taxable wages lost to injured workers. When the tax status of benefits is considered, after-tax wage replacement rates are significantly higher than before-tax rates, approaching two-thirds for our conservative measure based on income while working, but still below 50 percent for full losses including time out of work.

- We observed continuing wage loss in the last year of our data, but few of the claimants were still eligible to receive benefits. We simulated the effect of continued wage loss for 10 years after the injury; the simulation lowered wage replacement rates by more than the tax adjustment raised them.

- We investigated how the benefit schedule adopted in the 1993 reforms would have affected benefits for our sample of workers injured in 1991–1993. The percentage of wage loss replaced by workers' compensation benefits would have increased from 48 to 53 percent, based on the conservative income while working, and from 38 to 42 percent, based on full lost wages. Measured against the two-thirds replacement criterion, the rates are still inadequate.

Injured workers may also receive compensation from other programs over the four to five years after the injury, such as Social Security Disability Insurance or Unemployment Insurance. The estimated replacement rates, therefore, do not necessarily reflect the replacement of income by all social insurance programs, only workers' compensation. To fully assess the financial consequences of a workplace injury, future research must also consider the availability of other income support programs.

5. ANALYSES OF DISABILITY RATINGS AND THE CLAIMS PROCESS

Our analyses of available workers' compensation databases provided a way to examine issues raised in the interviews. These analyses drew primarily on the Uniform Statistical Report claims database provided to us by the WCIRB. These data, which included hundreds of thousands of PPD claims made to insured employers from 1989 through 1994, account for about 70 percent of PPD claims but do not provide direct information about the PPD process among self-insured employers. We based additional analyses on data from the Disability Evaluation Unit of the Division of Workers' Compensation.

The broadest conclusion flowing from these data analyses is that the workers' compensation system faces two different sets of PPD claims that present divergent demands and problems. As Figure 4 suggests, by almost every measure California's PPD system is overwhelmingly a system for dealing with "minor" disabilities (defined as disability ratings below 25 percent): PPD claims with disability ratings under 25 account for 90 percent of PPD claims, 80 percent of medical benefits, 70 percent of indemnity benefits, and 60 percent of legal fees.

By almost every measure, California's PPD system is overwhelmingly a system for dealing with minor disabilities.

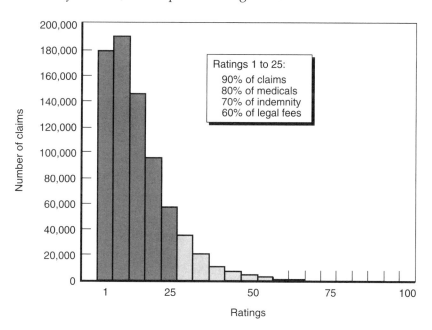

SOURCE: WCIRB Uniform Statistical Report database, 1989–1994 accident years.

Figure 4—The Vast Majority of PPD Claims Involve Low Ratings

Higher-rated PPD claims, described as "major" claims by the WCIRB, involve larger individual financial stakes, and their ratings present problems of inconsistency and subjectivity that trouble critics. But these major claims are exceptional; they do not represent what the workers' compensation system mostly does.

But both minor and major claims go through the same process—and delay.

Despite these differences, minor and major claims go through the same workers' compensation process and both types experience significant delays. Most minor claims take three or more years to resolve, even though minor claimants leave temporary disability within five months. Unfortunately, major claims take even longer. Because all PPD claims go through the same process, the cost of this process is particularly high in relation to the modest benefits for minor claims.

Our wage loss analysis provides further insights into the difference between high- and low-rated claims and examines the validity of the rating process for each type of claim. PPD claimants with the highest disability ratings should be those who suffer the greatest loss of ability to compete in an open labor market, i.e., those with the greatest wage losses. The wage loss study confirmed the general validity of ratings under the disability schedule. Among the small portion of claims with major injuries, disability ratings corresponded with wage loss. For example, applicants with the highest disability ratings, 36 to 99, had higher proportional wage losses than applicants with less seriously rated injuries, 21 to 35, who in turn had higher proportional wage losses than applicants with lower-rated injuries. Workers with higher disability ratings were less likely to return to or remain at work and, when at work, suffered greater losses in earnings.

Among minor injury claims, differences in disability ratings correspond poorly to wage loss.

However, the wage loss study also showed that among minor injury claims—the overwhelming bulk of PPD claims—there is little validity to disability ratings: Differences in disability ratings corresponded poorly with wage loss. As Table 1 shows, over the period of five years after the injury, there is very little relationship between the percentage of wage loss and disability rating for the lowest disability rating categories, 1–5, 6–10, and 11–20.

Even among the lowest disability ratings—ratings less than five—wage losses were large: On average, over the five years after the injury these claimants lost between 18 and 30 percent of earnings. The lack of a relationship between disability rating and wage loss for low-rated claims indicates that the present schedule poorly measures California's statutory basis for determining disability ratings—the loss of ability to compete. For the vast majority of claims, the validity of the disability rating is questionable.

Table 1

RELATIONSHIP BETWEEN DISABILITY RATING AND WAGE LOSS

Disability Rating	Control and Worker at Work		Control and Worker at Work and Out of Work	
	Percentage of Wage Loss over 5 Years	Percentage of Wage Loss Replaced by Workers' Compensation Benefits	Percentage of Wage Loss over 5 Years	Percentage of Wage Loss Replaced by Workers' Compensation Benefits
	20	48	40	38
1–5	18	14	30	12
6–10	17	29	29	21
11–20	17	51	32	35
21–35	25	68	46	51
36–99	34	84	69	48

Furthermore, the adequacy of workers' compensation benefits differed between major and minor claims. As Table 1 illustrates, workers' compensation benefits most fully replaced lost wages for claimants with major injuries, i.e., those with disability ratings above 20. Although applicants in this group experienced the greatest amount of lost work time, they also received the most benefits. If wage loss is measured conservatively, based on income while working, benefits replace more than the two-thirds goal. If wage loss is calculated fully to include time away from work, benefits replace about 50 percent of wage loss.

Workers' compensation benefits most fully replace lost wages for claimants with major injuries.

In contrast, workers' compensation benefits compensated only a small fraction of wage loss for the vast majority of workers with minor permanent partial disabilities. For instance, for workers with disability ratings 1–5, only 12 to 14 percent of wage loss is replaced. This group, along with all PPD applicants with disability ratings below 16, has not received an increase in PPD benefits since 1984.

Benefits compensate less than half the wage loss experienced by the vast majority of workers with minor disability claims.

Perhaps the most surprising and poorly understood result of our research is the large wage loss among workers with low-rated claims. We do not know if the injuries and resulting disabilities associated with the low ratings are in fact not as minor as the ratings suggest or, alternatively, if even modest workplace injuries may have consequences far beyond the resulting impairment. For example, these substantial wage losses might result from stigma associated with claiming permanent partial disability, disruption of career development, or strain on worker-employer relations because of the injury and/or claim. Similar wage losses have been found in studies of the effects of layoffs. Given the level of wage losses for workers with low disability ratings and the uncertainty about why the losses are so large, these findings should be examined through further empirical investigation of this issue.

6. POLICY RECOMMENDATIONS

The qualitative and quantitative analyses described above provided the basis for the policy recommendations we made to the Commission on Health and Safety and Workers' Compensation.

We recommended that a task force be created to improve the validity, reliability, and efficiency of the PPD ratings process and the disability schedule used in that process. The task force should include a working group of persons with experience, technical skills, and the analytic perspective needed to consider and implement changes in the treatment of PPD claims in California. The task force should work in conjunction with and under the direction of a policy group that represents important interest groups in the workers' compensation community and that can help facilitate changes recommended by the task force.

We recommended a task force to improve the PPD ratings process and the disability schedule.

We urged the task force to consider several policies suggested by our research findings. We briefly describe each of these below.

Implement an elective fast-track system for compensating minor PPD claims. The most consistent set of results in our research argues for adopting different procedures to deal more efficiently and fairly with minor PPD claims. Claims with disability ratings under 20 or 25 dominate the PPD claims volume, the indemnity and medical paid, and processing costs. Despite the relatively low stakes involved in each of these cases, they take years to resolve, clogging the courts and the caseloads for insurers, self-insured employers, and third-party administrators. Parties spend a great deal of money fighting over small differences in benefits, and the consequent congestion delays resolution of other, more serious claims, disadvantaging all injured workers. Furthermore, the resulting, usually modest differences in benefits are only weakly related to the real wage losses that workers sustain.

A fast-track system for PPD claims would provide fixed and certain payments to claimants who meet certain criteria.

The proposed fast-track system could create a simple, objectively based administrative system to provide fixed and certain payments to claimants who meet certain specified criteria. Applicants could elect either the present system or the simplified administrative fast-track system and benefit levels would be similar under either system. Such a system should speed claims resolution for the vast majority of PPD claims.

The fast-track option would be available only to claimants with claims rated below 20 or 25, and only to those who have injuries that are acknowledged to be work-related. Employers could force a summary process to determine whether the injury was related to the worker's employment. The summary process would be handled quickly to ensure that applicants are not denied the principal advantage of the fast-track system—early resolution of their claims.

The fast track would be based on a schedule listing specific injuries that are documented by specific objective medical findings. Each scheduled injury would be associated with a non-negotiable flat payment; an applicant's eligibility for payment within any category would be determined by an evaluation from a treating doctor.

If an employer disputed the treating doctor's evaluation, the claim would be handled as it is now, by a panel of three physicians who are Qualified Medical Examiners. If an applicant did not accept the panel's evaluation, he/she could withdraw from the fast track and proceed along the normal workers' compensation track. Payment of the fast-track amount would serve as a final resolution of the indemnity rights for a particular claim.

The task force should be responsible for determining both the categories of injuries in the fast-track schedule and the payment amounts. Payment schedules should be developed using current payment patterns as well as information generated by the wage loss study about actual wage losses associated with particular injury types.

Claimants should be able to use applicant attorneys for counseling and advice regarding whether to choose the fast track. The amount of compensation for such services should be set so that attorneys are financially indifferent to an applicant's choice of track. This principle implies a lower rate of compensation for advising applicants under the fast-track system, since attorneys will be able to represent many more fast-track claims than those requiring ordinary litigation.

To implement the fast-track system, the task force will need to address a number of technical and strategic issues—for example, identifying injury categories that can be characterized by objective medical findings and that historically have received relatively homogeneous PPD payments. The task force will also need to consider how the availability of a fast, easy, and certain payment program will affect the number of workers who apply for PPD benefits.

The wage-loss approach could establish an empirically based link between types of injuries and wage loss.

Revise the PPD schedule based on a wage loss approach. We recommend the development of an empirically derived disability schedule based on an expansion of our wage loss study. This would require supplementing current limited information about medical conditions and occupations. Since the objective of an empirically derived workers' compensation schedule is to identify and appropriately weight each factor that might be related to an injured worker's wage loss, data should be collected for all elements of the present PPD schedule that the task force believes might be related to a worker's wage loss.

The *American Medical Association Guides* provides a potentially valuable source for identifying medical findings, tests, and other medical judgments that might appropriately be considered as elements of the revised schedule. Using the *Guides* to identify elements to include in the wage loss study does not suggest that the *Guides* should be adopted in their entirety. Finally, the task force should work with experienced raters, adjusters, and applicants' lawyers to identify other medical matters routinely used to evaluate and rate claims under the PPD schedule.

Revisions of the disability schedule should be sensitive to how such changes might affect the return of injured workers to meaningful employment as well as their retention on the job. As we suggest below, California should develop policies aimed at increasing return and retention of injured workers.

If California develops policies that are effective in returning and retaining injured workers, the relationships between particular injuries and wage losses are likely to change over time. Consequently, the task force, the Division of Workers' Compensation, or another appropriate entity should periodically update the wage loss study, test the validity of the then current schedule, and revise it as necessary.

Develop and distribute a database on closed PPD claims. The task force could facilitate more informed decisions by claimants and more consistent settlements by obtaining and providing claims-level data that track how claims are being resolved in the PPD system. These data would provide feedback to lawyers, applicants, employers, and insurance adjusters about historical patterns in claims resolution and could guide decisionmaking and help set reasonable expectations about resolving new claims. The availability of these sorts of data will help ensure a more informed and consistent set of practices and resolutions under the workers' compensation system, operating under either the current or a revised wage-loss-based schedule.

Information on closed PPD claims would facilitate claimant decisionmaking and promote more consistent settlements.

Review strategies for increasing return to work. The task force can draw upon both the wage loss study as well as a possible follow-up study of applicants and employers to better understand why injured workers have a low rate of return to work and why they experience episodic periods of employment and unemployment after their return. The task force should consider strategies for increasing return to work and employment stability after injury. As part of this consideration, the task force should monitor the effects of statutory attempts in other states to encourage return to work.

Strategies for increasing return to work should reflect the experience of other states with such policies.

Improve the consistency and predictability of the rating process. Many people we interviewed expressed concern about the consistency and predictability of disability ratings. Such concerns seem inevitable given any process that attempts to impose simple, standardized ratings upon the complex variety of injuries and work requirements involved with workplace injuries. Our research suggests that problems of rating consistency and predictability exist in the current California disability rating schedule and are more severe for low-rated claims. This by itself can undermine the validity of the rating process.

Testing the consistency of raters in the DEU would produce multiple benefits.

However, the Division of Workers' Compensation and the DEU can improve the consistency and predictability of the rating process—and others' confidence in that process—by instituting routine procedures for testing the consistency of DEU raters. Such reliability checks would provide a measure of the overall reliability and consistency of the DEU rating process, identify troublesome areas of the disability schedule or types of claims that have comparatively low rating consistency, identify raters whose practices differ from those of most other raters, and provide the basis of materials used to train raters.

In addition to the proposals discussed above, we also recommended that the Division of Workers' Compensation undertake several initiatives, including the following:

- Improve the utility of medical evaluations by developing mandated procedures for electronic filings of medical reports and developing, with the Industrial Medical Council, guides to aid doctors through the process of evaluating claims.

- Expedite claims resolution by mandating electronic filing of documents with the Workers' Compensation Appeals Board, the court system used to process litigated workers' compensation claims.

We believe that most of these policy recommendations can be implemented in ways that produce general and shared benefits across the broad communities interested in California's workers' compensation system. Historically, workers' compensation in California has been highly politicized, with changes often more a matter of coalescence of several interest groups who impose a decision upon others. Our research points the way toward changes that would produce more efficient, appropriate, and rational treatment of workers who have permanent disabilities and suggests that the benefits of such changes might be shared among parties who, although adversaries in individual cases, share common interests in a fairer and less costly system. Our discussions with system participants and stakeholders suggest that there is a willingness to consider the reforms we have suggested and to share their possible benefits.

ICJ PUBLICATIONS

Outcomes

General

Carroll, S. J., with N. M. Pace, *Assessing the Effects of Tort Reforms*, R-3554-ICJ, 1987. $7.50.

Galanter, M., B. Garth, D. Hensler, and F. K. Zemans, *How to Improve Civil Justice Policy*, RP-282. (Reprinted from *Judicature*, Vol. 77, No. 4, January/February 1994.) Free.

Hensler, D. R., *Summary of Research Results on the Tort Liability System*, P-7210-ICJ, 1986. (Testimony before the Committee on Commerce, Science, and Transportation, United States Senate, February 1986.) $4.00.

_____ , *Trends in California Tort Liability Litigation*, P-7287-ICJ, 1987. (Testimony before the Select Committee on Insurance, California State Assembly, October 1987.) $4.00.

_____ , *Researching Civil Justice: Problems and Pitfalls*, P-7604-ICJ, 1988. (Reprinted from *Law and Contemporary Problems*, Vol. 51, No. 3, Summer 1988.) $4.00.

_____ , *Reading the Tort Litigation Tea Leaves: What's Going on in the Civil Liability System?* RP-226. (Reprinted from *The Justice System Journal*, Vol. 16, No. 2, 1993.) Free.

_____ , *Why We Don't Know More About the Civil Justice System—and What We Could Do About It*, RP-363, 1995. (Reprinted from *USC Law*, Fall 1994.) Free.

Hensler, D. R., and E. Moller, *Trends in Punitive Damages: Preliminary Data from Cook County, Illinois, and San Francisco, California*, DRU-1014-ICJ, 1995. Free.

Hensler, D. R., M. E. Vaiana, J. S. Kakalik, and M. A. Peterson, *Trends in Tort Litigation: The Story Behind the Statistics*, R-3583-ICJ, 1987. $4.00.

Hill, P. T., and D. L. Madey, *Educational Policymaking Through the Civil Justice System*, R-2904-ICJ, 1982. $4.00.

Lipson, A. J., *California Enacts Prejudgment Interest: A Case Study of Legislative Action*, N-2096-ICJ, 1984. $4.00.

Moller, E., *Trends in Punitive Damages: Preliminary Data from California*, DRU-1059-ICJ, 1995. Free.

Shubert, G. H., *Some Observations on the Need for Tort Reform*, P-7189-ICJ, 1986. (Testimony before the National Conference of State Legislatures, January 1986.) $4.00.

_____ , *Changes in the Tort System: Helping Inform the Policy Debate*, P-7241-ICJ, 1986. $4.00.

Jury Verdicts

Bailis, D. S., and R. J. MacCoun, *Estimating Liability Risks with the Media as Your Guide*, RP-606, 1996. (Reprinted from *Law and Human Behavior*, Vol. 20, No. 4, 1996, pp. 419–429.) Free.

Carroll, S. J., *Jury Awards and Prejudgment Interest in Tort Cases*, N-1994-ICJ, 1983. $4.00.

_____ , *Punitive Damages in Financial Injury Jury Verdicts*, CT-143, June 1997. (Written statement delivered on June 24, 1997, to the Judiciary Committee of the United States Senate.) $5.00.

Chin, A., and M. A. Peterson, *Deep Pockets, Empty Pockets: Who Wins in Cook County Jury Trials*, R-3249-ICJ, 1985. $10.00.

Dertouzos, J. N., E. Holland, and P. A. Ebener, *The Legal and Economic Consequences of Wrongful Termination*, R-3602-ICJ, 1988. $7.50.

Hensler, D. R., *Summary of Research Results on the Tort Liability System*, P-7210-ICJ, 1986. (Testimony before the Committee on Commerce, Science, and Transportation, United States Senate, February 1986.) $4.00.

Hensler, D. R., and E. Moller, *Trends in Punitive Damages: Preliminary Data from Cook County, Illinois, and San Francisco, California*, DRU-1014-ICJ, 1995. Free.

MacCoun, R. J., *Getting Inside the Black Box: Toward a Better Understanding of Civil Jury Behavior*, N-2671-ICJ, 1987. $4.00.

_____ , *Experimental Research on Jury Decisionmaking*, R-3832-ICJ, 1989. (Reprinted from *Science*, Vol. 244, June 1989.) $4.00.

_____ , *Inside the Black Box: What Empirical Research Tells Us About Decisionmaking by Civil Juries*, RP-238, 1993. (Reprinted from Robert E. Litan, ed., *Verdict: Assessing the Civil Jury System*, The Brookings Institution, 1993.) Free.

_____ , *Is There a "Deep-Pocket" Bias in the Tort System?* IP-130, October 1993. Free.

_____ , *Blaming Others to a Fault?* RP-286. (Reprinted from *Chance*, Vol. 6, No. 4, Fall 1993.) Free.

_____ , *Improving Jury Comprehension in Criminal and Civil Trials*, CT-136, July 1995. $5.00.

Moller, E., *Trends in Punitive Damages: Preliminary Data from California*, DRU-1059-ICJ, 1995. Free.

_____ , *Trends in Civil Jury Verdicts Since 1985*, MR-694-ICJ, 1996. $15.00.

Moller, E., N. M. Pace, and S. J. Carroll, *Punitive Damages in Financial Injury Jury Verdicts*, MR-888-ICJ, 1997. $9.00.

_____ , *Punitive Damages in Financial Injury Jury Verdicts: Executive Summary*, MR-889-ICJ, 1997. $15.00.

Peterson, M. A., *Compensation of Injuries: Civil Jury Verdicts in Cook County*, R-3011-ICJ, 1984. $7.50.

_____ , *Punitive Damages: Preliminary Empirical Findings*, N-2342-ICJ, 1985. $4.00.

_____ , *Summary of Research Results: Trends and Patterns in Civil Jury Verdicts*, P-7222-ICJ, 1986. (Testimony before the Subcommittee on Oversight, Committee on Ways and Means, United States House of Representatives, March 1986.) $4.00.

_____ , *Civil Juries in the 1980s: Trends in Jury Trials and Verdicts in California and Cook County, Illinois*, R-3466-ICJ, 1987. $7.50.

Peterson, M. A., and G. L. Priest, *The Civil Jury: Trends in Trials and Verdicts, Cook County, Illinois, 1960–1979*, R-2881-ICJ, 1982. $7.50.

Peterson, M. A., S. Sarma, and M. G. Shanley, *Punitive Damages: Empirical Findings*, R-3311-ICJ, 1987. $7.50.

Selvin, M., and L. Picus, *The Debate over Jury Performance: Observations from a Recent Asbestos Case*, R-3479-ICJ, 1987. $10.00.

Shanley, M. G., and M. A. Peterson, *Comparative Justice: Civil Jury Verdicts in San Francisco and Cook Counties, 1959–1980*, R-3006-ICJ, 1983. $7.50.

_____ , *Posttrial Adjustments to Jury Awards*, R-3511-ICJ, 1987. $7.50.

Costs of Dispute Resolution

Dunworth, T., and J. S. Kakalik, *Preliminary Observations on Implementation of the Pilot Program of the Civil Justice Reform Act of 1990*, RP-361, 1995. (Reprinted from *Stanford Law Review*, Vol. 46, No. 6, July 1994.) Free.

Hensler, D. R., *Does ADR Really Save Money? The Jury's Still Out*, RP-327, 1994. (Reprinted from *The National Law Journal*, April 11, 1994.) Free.

Hensler, D. R., M. E. Vaiana, J. S. Kakalik, and M. A. Peterson, *Trends in Tort Litigation: The Story Behind the Statistics*, R-3583-ICJ, 1987. $4.00.

Kakalik, J. S., and A. E. Robyn, *Costs of the Civil Justice System: Court Expenditures for Processing Tort Cases*, R-2888-ICJ, 1982. $7.50.

Kakalik, J. S., and R. L. Ross, *Costs of the Civil Justice System: Court Expenditures for Various Types of Civil Cases*, R-2985-ICJ, 1983. $10.00.

Kakalik, J. S., P. A. Ebener, W. L. F. Felstiner, and M. G. Shanley, *Costs of Asbestos Litigation*, R-3042-ICJ, 1983. $4.00.

Kakalik, J. S., P. A. Ebener, W. L. F. Felstiner, G. W. Haggstrom, and M. G. Shanley, *Variation in Asbestos Litigation Compensation and Expenses*, R-3132-ICJ, 1984. $7.50.

Kakalik, J. S., and N. M. Pace, *Costs and Compensation Paid in Tort Litigation*, R-3391-ICJ, 1986. $15.00.

_____ , *Costs and Compensation Paid in Tort Litigation*, P-7243-ICJ, 1986. (Testimony before the Subcommittee on Trade, Productivity, and Economic Growth, Joint Economic Committee of the Congress, July 1986.) $4.00.

Kakalik, J. S., E. M. King, M. Traynor, P. A. Ebener, and L. Picus, *Costs and Compensation Paid in Aviation Accident Litigation*, R-3421-ICJ, 1988. $10.00.

Kakalik, J. S., M. Selvin, and N. M. Pace, *Averting Gridlock: Strategies for Reducing Civil Delay in the Los Angeles Superior Court*, R-3762-ICJ, 1990. $10.00.

Kakalik, J. S., T. Dunworth, L. A. Hill, D. McCaffrey, M. Oshiro, N. M. Pace, and M. E. Vaiana, *Just, Speedy, and Inexpensive? An Evaluation of Judicial Case Management Under the Civil Justice Reform Act*, MR-800-ICJ, 1996. $8.00.

_____ , *Implementation of the Civil Justice Reform Act in Pilot and Comparison Districts*, MR-801-ICJ, 1996. $20.00.

_____ , *An Evaluation of Judicial Case Management Under the Civil Justice Reform Act*, MR-802-ICJ, 1996. $20.00.

_____ , *An Evaluation of Mediation and Early Neutral Evaluation Under the Civil Justice Reform Act*, MR-803-ICJ, 1996. $20.00.

Lind, E. A., *Arbitrating High-Stakes Cases: An Evaluation of Court-Annexed Arbitration in a United States District Court*, R-3809-ICJ, 1990. $10.00.

MacCoun, R. J., E. A. Lind, D. R. Hensler, D. L. Bryant, and P. A. Ebener, *Alternative Adjudication: An Evaluation of the New Jersey Automobile Arbitration Program*, R-3676-ICJ, 1988. $10.00.

Peterson, M. A., *New Tools for Reducing Civil Litigation Expenses*, R-3013-ICJ, 1983. $4.00.

Priest, G. L., *Regulating the Content and Volume of Litigation: An Economic Analysis*, R-3084-ICJ, 1983. $4.00.

Dispute Resolution

Court Delay

Adler, J. W., W. L. F. Felstiner, D. R. Hensler, and M. A. Peterson, *The Pace of Litigation: Conference Proceedings*, R-2922-ICJ, 1982. $10.00.

Dunworth, T., and J. S. Kakalik, *Preliminary Observations on Implementation of the Pilot Program of the Civil Justice Reform Act of 1990*, RP-361, 1995. (Reprinted from *Stanford Law Review*, Vol. 46, No. 6, July 1994.) Free.

Dunworth, T., and N. M. Pace, *Statistical Overview of Civil Litigation in the Federal Courts*, R-3885-ICJ, 1990. $7.50.

Ebener, P. A., *Court Efforts to Reduce Pretrial Delay: A National Inventory*, R-2732-ICJ, 1981. $10.00.

Kakalik, J. S., *Just, Speedy, and Inexpensive? Judicial Case Management Under the Civil Justice Reform Act*, RP-635, 1997. (Reprinted from *Judicature*, Vol. 80, No. 4, January–February 1997, pp. 184–189.) Free.

Kakalik, J. S., M. Selvin, and N. M. Pace, *Averting Gridlock: Strategies for Reducing Civil Delay in the Los Angeles Superior Court*, R-3762-ICJ, 1990. $10.00.

_____ , *Strategies for Reducing Civil Delay in the Los Angeles Superior Court: Technical Appendixes*, N-2988-ICJ, 1990. $10.00.

Kakalik, J. S., T. Dunworth, L. A. Hill, D. McCaffrey, M. Oshiro, N. M. Pace, and M. E. Vaiana, *Just, Speedy, and Inexpensive? An Evaluation of Judicial Case Management Under the Civil Justice Reform Act*, MR-800-ICJ, 1996. $8.00.

_____ , *Implementation of the Civil Justice Reform Act in Pilot and Comparison Districts*, MR-801-ICJ, 1996. $20.00.

_____ , *An Evaluation of Judicial Case Management Under the Civil Justice Reform Act*, MR-802-ICJ, 1996. $20.00.

_____ , *An Evaluation of Mediation and Early Neutral Evaluation Under the Civil Justice Reform Act*, MR-803-ICJ, 1996. $20.00.

Lind, E. A., *Arbitrating High-Stakes Cases: An Evaluation of Court-Annexed Arbitration in a United States District Court*, R-3809-ICJ, 1990. $10.00.

MacCoun, R. J., E. A. Lind, D. R. Hensler, D. L. Bryant, and P. A. Ebener, *Alternative Adjudication: An Evaluation of the New Jersey Automobile Arbitration Program*, R-3676-ICJ, 1988. $10.00.

Resnik, J., *Managerial Judges*, R-3002-ICJ, 1982. (Reprinted from the *Harvard Law Review*, Vol. 96, No. 374, December 1982.) $7.50.

Selvin, M., and P. A. Ebener, *Managing the Unmanageable: A History of Civil Delay in the Los Angeles Superior Court*, R-3165-ICJ, 1984. $15.00.

Alternative Dispute Resolution

Adler, J. W., D. R. Hensler, and C. E. Nelson, with the assistance of G. J. Rest, *Simple Justice: How Litigants Fare in the Pittsburgh Court Arbitration Program*, R-3071-ICJ, 1983. $15.00.

Bryant, D. L., *Judicial Arbitration in California: An Update*, N-2909-ICJ, 1989. $4.00.

Ebener, P. A., and D. R. Betancourt, *Court-Annexed Arbitration: The National Picture*, N-2257-ICJ, 1985. $25.00.

Hensler, D. R., *Court-Annexed Arbitration in the State Trial Court System*, P-6963-ICJ, 1984. (Testimony before the Judiciary Committee Subcommittee on Courts, United States Senate, February 1984.) $4.00.

_____ , *Reforming the Civil Litigation Process: How Court Arbitration Can Help*, P-7027-ICJ, 1984. (Reprinted from the *New Jersey Bell Journal*, August 1984.) $4.00.

_____ , *What We Know and Don't Know About Court-Administered Arbitration*, N-2444-ICJ, 1986. $4.00.

_____ , *Court-Ordered Arbitration: An Alternative View*, RP-103, 1992. (Reprinted from *The University of Chicago Legal Forum*, Vol. 1990, 1990.) Free.

_____ , *Science in the Court: Is There a Role for Alternative Dispute Resolution?* RP-109, 1992. (Reprinted from *Law and Contemporary Problems*, Vol. 54, No. 3, Summer 1991.) Free.

_____ , *Does ADR Really Save Money? The Jury's Still Out*, RP-327, 1994. (Reprinted from *The National Law Journal*, April 11, 1994.) Free.

_____ , *A Glass Half Full, a Glass Half Empty: The Use of Alternative Dispute Resolution in Mass Personal Injury Litigation*, RP-446, 1995. (Reprinted from *Texas Law Review*, Vol. 73, No. 7, June 1995.) Free.

Hensler, D. R., A. J. Lipson, and E. S. Rolph, *Judicial Arbitration in California: The First Year*, R-2733-ICJ, 1981. $10.00.

_____ , *Judicial Arbitration in California: The First Year: Executive Summary*, R-2733/1-ICJ, 1981. $4.00.

Hensler, D. R., and J. W. Adler, with the assistance of G. J. Rest, *Court-Administered Arbitration: An Alternative for Consumer Dispute Resolution*, N-1965-ICJ, 1983. $4.00.

Kakalik, J. S., T. Dunworth, L. A. Hill, D. McCaffrey, M. Oshiro, N. M. Pace, and M. E. Vaiana, *An Evaluation of Mediation and Early Neutral Evaluation Under the Civil Justice Reform Act*, MR-803-ICJ, 1996. $20.00.

Lind, E. A., *Arbitrating High-Stakes Cases: An Evaluation of Court-Annexed Arbitration in a United States District Court*, R-3809-ICJ, 1990. $10.00.

Lind, E. A., R. J. MacCoun, P. A. Ebener, W. L. F. Felstiner, D. R. Hensler, J. Resnik, and T. R. Tyler, *The Perception of Justice: Tort Litigants' Views of Trial, Court-Annexed Arbitration, and Judicial Settlement Conferences*, R-3708-ICJ, 1989. $7.50.

MacCoun, R. J., *Unintended Consequences of Court Arbitration: A Cautionary Tale from New Jersey*, RP-134, 1992. (Reprinted from *The Justice System Journal*, Vol. 14, No. 2, 1991.) Free.

MacCoun, R. J., E. A. Lind, D. R. Hensler, D. L. Bryant, and P. A. Ebener, *Alternative Adjudication: An Evaluation of the New Jersey Automobile Arbitration Program*, R-3676-ICJ, 1988. $10.00.

MacCoun, R. J., E. A. Lind, and T. R. Tyler, *Alternative Dispute Resolution in Trial and Appellate Courts*, RP-117, 1992. (Reprinted from *Handbook of Psychology and Law*, 1992.) Free.

Moller, E., E. S. Rolph, and P. Ebener, *Private Dispute Resolution in the Banking Industry*, MR-259-ICJ, 1993. $13.00.

Resnik, J., *Many Doors? Closing Doors? Alternative Dispute Resolution and Adjudication*, RP-439, 1995. (Reprinted from *The Ohio State Journal on Dispute Resolution*, Vol. 10, No. 2, 1995.) Free.

Rolph, E. S., *Introducing Court-Annexed Arbitration: A Policymaker's Guide*, R-3167-ICJ, 1984. $10.00.

Rolph, E. S., and D. R. Hensler, *Court-Ordered Arbitration: The California Experience*, N-2186-ICJ, 1984. $4.00.

Rolph, E. S., and E. Moller, *Evaluating Agency Alternative Dispute Resolution Programs: A Users' Guide to Data Collection and Use*, MR-534-ACUS/ICJ, 1995. $13.00.

Rolph, E. S., E. Moller, and L. Petersen, *Escaping the Courthouse: Private Alternative Dispute Resolution in Los Angeles*, MR-472-JRHD/ICJ, 1994. $15.00.

Special Issues

Kritzer, H. M., W. L. F. Felstiner, A. Sarat, and D. M. Trubek, *The Impact of Fee Arrangement on Lawyer Effort*, P-7180-ICJ, 1986. $4.00.

Priest, G. L., *Regulating the Content and Volume of Litigation: An Economic Analysis*, R-3084-ICJ, 1983. $4.00.

Priest, G. L., and B. Klein, *The Selection of Disputes for Litigation*, R-3032-ICJ, 1984. $7.50.

Resnik, J., *Managerial Judges*, R-3002-ICJ, 1982. (Reprinted from the *Harvard Law Review*, Vol. 96, No. 374, December 1982.) $7.50.

_____ , *Failing Faith: Adjudicatory Procedure in Decline*, P-7272-ICJ, 1987. (Reprinted from the *University of Chicago Law Review*, Vol. 53, No. 2, 1986.) $7.50.

_____ , *Due Process: A Public Dimension*, P-7418-ICJ, 1988. (Reprinted from the *University of Florida Law Review*, Vol. 39, No. 2, 1987.) $4.00.

_____ , *Judging Consent*, P-7419-ICJ, 1988. (Reprinted from the *University of Chicago Legal Forum*, Vol. 1987.) $7.50.

_____ , *From "Cases" to "Litigation,"* RP-110, 1992. (Reprinted from *Law and Contemporary Problems*, Vol. 54, No. 3, Summer 1991.) Free.

_____ , *Whose Judgment? Vacating Judgments, Preferences for Settlement, and the Role of Adjudication at the Close of the Twentieth Century*, RP-364, 1995. (Reprinted from *UCLA Law Review*, Vol. 41, No. 6, August 1994.) Free.

Areas of Liability

Auto Personal Injury Compensation

Abrahamse, A., and S. J. Carroll, *The Effects of a Choice Auto Insurance Plan on Insurance Costs*, MR-540-ICJ, 1995. $13.00.

_____ , *The Effects of a Choice Automobile Insurance Plan Under Consideration by the Joint Economic Committee of the United States Congress*, DRU-1609-ICJ, April 1997. Free.

_____ , *The Effects of Proposition 213 on the Costs of Auto Insurance in California*, IP-157, September 1996. Free.

Carroll, S. J., *Effects of an Auto-Choice Automobile Insurance Plan on Costs and Premiums*, CT-141-1, March 1997. (Written statement delivered on March 19, 1997, to the Joint Economic Committee of the United States Congress.) $5.00.

_____ , *Effects of a Choice Automobile Insurance Plan on Costs and Premiums: Testimony Presented to the Senate Commerce, Science, and Transportation Committee, July 1997*, CT-144, July 1997. (Written statement delivered on July 17, 1997, to the Commerce, Science, and Transportation Committee of the United States Senate.) $5.00.

Carroll, S. J., and A. Abrahamse, *The Effects of a Proposed No-Fault Plan on the Costs of Auto Insurance in California: An Updated Analysis*, IP-146-1, January 1996. Free.

Carroll, S. J., and J. S. Kakalik, *No-Fault Approaches to Compensating Auto Accident Victims*, RP-229, 1993. (Reprinted from *The Journal of Risk and Insurance*, Vol. 60, No. 2, 1993.) Free.

Carroll, S. J., A. Abrahamse, and M. E. Vaiana, *The Costs of Excess Medical Claims for Automobile Personal Injuries*, DB-139-ICJ, 1995. $6.00.

Carroll, S. J., J. S. Kakalik, N. M. Pace, and J. L. Adams, *No-Fault Approaches to Compensating People Injured in Automobile Accidents*, R-4019-ICJ, 1991. $20.00.

Carroll, S. J., and J. S. Kakalik, with D. Adamson, *No-Fault Automobile Insurance: A Policy Perspective*, R-4019/1-ICJ, 1991. $4.00.

Hammitt, J. K., *Automobile Accident Compensation, Volume II, Payments by Auto Insurers*, R-3051-ICJ, 1985. $10.00.

Hammitt, J. K., and J. E. Rolph, *Limiting Liability for Automobile Accidents: Are No-Fault Tort Thresholds Effective?* N-2418-ICJ, 1985. $4.00.

Hammitt, J. K., R. L. Houchens, S. S. Polin, and J. E. Rolph, *Automobile Accident Compensation: Volume IV, State Rules*, R-3053-ICJ, 1985. $7.50.

Houchens, R. L., *Automobile Accident Compensation: Volume III, Payments from All Sources*, R-3052-ICJ, 1985. $7.50.

MacCoun, R. J., E. A. Lind, D. R. Hensler, D. L. Bryant, and P. A. Ebener, *Alternative Adjudication: An Evaluation of the New Jersey Automobile Arbitration Program*, R-3676-ICJ, 1988. $10.00.

O'Connell, J., S. J. Carroll, M. Horowitz, and A. Abrahamse, *Consumer Choice in the Auto Insurance Market*, RP-254, 1994. (Reprinted from the *Maryland Law Review*, Vol. 52, 1993.) Free.

O'Connell, J., S. J. Carroll, M. Horowitz, A. F. Abrahamse, and P. Jamieson, *The Comparative Costs of Allowing Consumer Choice for Auto Insurance in All Fifty States*, RP-518, 1996. Free.

O'Connell, J., S. J. Carroll, M. Horowitz, A. Abrahamse, and D. Kaiser, *The Costs of Consumer Choice for Auto Insurance in States Without No-Fault Insurance*, RP-442, 1995. (Reprinted from *Maryland Law Review*, Vol. 54, No. 2, 1995.) Free.

Rolph, J. E., with J. K. Hammitt, R. L. Houchens, and S. S. Polin, *Automobile Accident Compensation: Volume I, Who Pays How Much How Soon?* R-3050-ICJ, 1985. $4.00.

Asbestos

Hensler, D. R., *Resolving Mass Toxic Torts: Myths and Realities*, P-7631-ICJ, 1990. (Reprinted from the *University of Illinois Law Review*, Vol. 1989, No. 1, 1989.) $4.00.

_____ , *Asbestos Litigation in the United States: A Brief Overview*, P-7776-ICJ, 1992. (Testimony before the Courts and Judicial Administration Subcommittee, United States House Judiciary Committee, October 1991.) $4.00.

_____ , *Assessing Claims Resolution Facilities: What We Need to Know*, RP-107, 1992. (Reprinted from *Law and Contemporary Problems*, Vol. 53, No. 4, Autumn 1990.) Free.

_____ , *Fashioning a National Resolution of Asbestos Personal Injury Litigation: A Reply to Professor Brickman*, RP-114, 1992. (Reprinted from *Cardozo Law Review*, Vol. 13, No. 6, April 1992.) Free.

Hensler, D. R., W. L. F. Felstiner, M. Selvin, and P. A. Ebener, *Asbestos in the Courts: The Challenge of Mass Toxic Torts*, R-3324-ICJ, 1985. $10.00.

Kakalik, J. S., P. A. Ebener, W. L. F. Felstiner, and M. G. Shanley, *Costs of Asbestos Litigation*, R-3042-ICJ, 1983. $4.00.

Kakalik, J. S., P. A. Ebener, W. L. F. Felstiner, G. W. Haggstrom, and M. G. Shanley, *Variation in Asbestos Litigation Compensation and Expenses*, R-3132-ICJ, 1984. $7.50.

Peterson, M. A., *Giving Away Money: Comparative Comments on Claims Resolution Facilities*, RP-108, 1992. (Reprinted from *Law and Contemporary Problems*, Vol. 53, No. 4, Autumn 1990.) Free.

Peterson, M. A., and M. Selvin, *Resolution of Mass Torts: Toward a Framework for Evaluation of Aggregative Procedures*, N-2805-ICJ, 1988. $7.50.

_____ , *Mass Justice: The Limited and Unlimited Power of Courts*, RP-116, 1992. (Reprinted from *Law and Contemporary Problems*, No. 3, Summer 1991.) Free.

Selvin, M., and L. Picus, *The Debate over Jury Performance: Observations from a Recent Asbestos Case*, R-3479-ICJ, 1987. $10.00.

Aviation Accidents

Kakalik, J. S., E. M. King, M. Traynor, P. A. Ebener, and L. Picus, *Costs and Compensation Paid in Aviation Accident Litigation*, R-3421-ICJ, 1988. $10.00.

_____ , *Aviation Accident Litigation Survey: Data Collection Forms*, N-2773-ICJ, 1988. $7.50.

King, E. M., and J. P. Smith, *Computing Economic Loss in Cases of Wrongful Death*, R-3549-ICJ, 1988. $10.00.

_____ , *Economic Loss and Compensation in Aviation Accidents*, R-3551-ICJ, 1988. $10.00.

_____ , *Dispute Resolution Following Airplane Crashes*, R-3585-ICJ, 1988. $7.50.

Executive Summaries of the Aviation Accident Study, R-3684, 1988. $7.50.

Environment: California's Clean-Air Strategy

Dixon, L. S., and S. Garber, *California's Ozone-Reduction Strategy for Light-Duty Vehicles: Direct Costs, Direct Emission Effects and Market Responses*, MR-695-ICJ, 1996. $13.00.

_____ , *Economic Perspectives on Revising California's Zero-Emission Vehicle Mandate*, CT-137, March 1996. $5.00.

Dixon, L. S., S. Garber, and M. E. Vaiana, *California's Ozone-Reduction Strategy for Light-Duty Vehicles: An Economic Assessment*, MR-695/1-ICJ, 1996. $15.00.

_____ , *Making ZEV Policy Despite Uncertainty: An Annotated Briefing for the California Air Resources Board*, DRU-1266-1-ICJ, 1995. Free.

Environment: Superfund

Acton, J. P., *Understanding Superfund: A Progress Report*, R-3838-ICJ, 1989. $7.50.

Acton, J. P., and L. S. Dixon with D. Drezner, L. Hill, and S. McKenney, *Superfund and Transaction Costs: The Experiences of Insurers and Very Large Industrial Firms*, R-4132-ICJ, 1992. $7.50.

Dixon, L. S., *RAND Research on Superfund Transaction Costs: A Summary of Findings to Date*, CT-111, November 1993. $5.00.

_____ , *Fixing Superfund: The Effect of the Proposed Superfund Reform Act of 1994 on Transaction Costs*, MR-455-ICJ, 1994. $15.00.

_____ , *Superfund Liability Reform: Implications for Transaction Costs and Site Cleanup*, CT-125, 1995. $5.00.

Dixon, L. S., D. S. Drezner, and J. K. Hammitt, *Private-Sector Cleanup Expenditures and Transaction Costs at 18 Superfund Sites*, MR-204-EPA/RC, 1993. $13.00.

Reuter, P., *The Economic Consequences of Expanded Corporate Liability: An Exploratory Study*, N-2807-ICJ, 1988. $7.50.

Law and the Changing American Workplace

Darling-Hammond, L., and T. J. Kniesner, *The Law and Economics of Workers' Compensation*, R-2716-ICJ, 1980. $7.50.

Dertouzos, J. N., E. Holland, and P. A. Ebener, *The Legal and Economic Consequences of Wrongful Termination*, R-3602-ICJ, 1988. $7.50.

Dertouzos, J. N., and L. A. Karoly, *Labor-Market Responses to Employer Liability*, R-3989-ICJ, 1992. $7.50.

Peterson, Mark A., Robert T. Reville, and Rachel Kaganoff Stern, with Peter Barth, *Compensating Permanent Workplace Injuries: A Study of the California System*, MR-920-ICJ, 1997. $20.00.

Stern, Rachel Kaganoff, Mark A. Peterson, Robert T. Reville, and Mary Vaiana, *Findings and Recommendations on California's Permanent Partial Disability System: Executive Summary*, MR-919-ICJ, 1997. $8.00.

Victor, R. B., *Workers' Compensation and Workplace Safety: The Nature of Employer Financial Incentives*, R-2979-ICJ, 1982. $7.50.

Victor, R. B., L. R. Cohen, and C. E. Phelps, *Workers' Compensation and Workplace Safety: Some Lessons from Economic Theory*, R-2918-ICJ, 1982. $7.50.

Medical Malpractice

Bailis, D. S., and R. J. MacCoun, *Estimating Liability Risks with the Media as Your Guide*, RP-606, 1996. (Reprinted from *Law and Human Behavior*, Vol. 20, No. 4, 1996, pp. 419–429.) Free.

Danzon, P. M., *Contingent Fees for Personal Injury Litigation*, R-2458-HCFA, 1980. $4.00.

_____ , *The Disposition of Medical Malpractice Claims*, R-2622-HCFA, 1980. $7.50.

_____ , *Why Are Malpractice Premiums So High—Or So Low?* R-2623-HCFA, 1980. $4.00.

_____ , *The Frequency and Severity of Medical Malpractice Claims*, R-2870-ICJ/HCFA, 1982. $7.50.

_____ , *New Evidence on the Frequency and Severity of Medical Malpractice Claims*, R-3410-ICJ, 1986. $4.00.

_____ , *The Effects of Tort Reform on the Frequency and Severity of Medical Malpractice Claims: A Summary of Research Results*, P-7211, 1986. (Testimony before the Committee on the Judiciary, United States Senate, March 1986.) $4.00.

Danzon, P. M., and L. A. Lillard, *The Resolution of Medical Malpractice Claims: Modeling the Bargaining Process*, R-2792-ICJ, 1982. $7.50.

_____ , *Settlement Out of Court: The Disposition of Medical Malpractice Claims*, P-6800, 1982. $4.00.

_____ , *The Resolution of Medical Malpractice Claims: Research Results and Policy Implications*, R-2793-ICJ, 1982. $4.00.

Kravitz, R. L. , J. E. Rolph, K. A. McGuigan, *Malpractice Claims Data as a Quality Improvement Tool: I. Epidemiology of Error in Four Specialties*, N-3448/1-RWJ, 1991. $4.00.

Lewis, E., and J. E. Rolph, *The Bad Apples? Malpractice Claims Experience of Physicians with a Surplus Lines Insurer*, P-7812, 1993. $4.00.

Rolph, E. S., *Health Care Delivery and Tort: Systems on a Collision Course?* Conference Proceedings, Dallas, June 1991, N-3524-ICJ, 1992. $10.00.

Rolph, J. E., *Some Statistical Evidence on Merit Rating in Medical Malpractice Insurance*, N-1725-HHS, 1981. $4.00.

_____ , *Merit Rating for Physicians' Malpractice Premiums: Only a Modest Deterrent*, N-3426-MT/RWJ/RC, 1991. $4.00.

Rolph, J. E., R. L. Kravitz, and K. A. McGuigan, *Malpractice Claims Data as a Quality Improvement Tool: II. Is Targeting Effective?* N-3448/2-RWJ, 1991. $4.00.

Williams, A. P., *Malpractice, Outcomes, and Appropriateness of Care*, P-7445, May 1988. $4.00.

Product Liability

Bailis, D. S., and R. J. MacCoun, *Estimating Liability Risks with the Media as Your Guide*, RP-606, 1996. (Reprinted from *Law and Human Behavior*, Vol. 20, No. 4, 1996, pp. 419–429.) Free.

Dunworth, T., *Product Liability and the Business Sector: Litigation Trends in Federal Courts*, R-3668-ICJ, 1988. $7.50.

Eads, G., and P. Reuter, *Designing Safer Products: Corporate Responses to Product Liability Law and Regulation*, R-3022-ICJ, 1983. $15.00.

_____ , *Designing Safer Products: Corporate Responses to Product Liability Law and Regulation*, P-7089-ICJ, 1985. (Reprinted from the *Journal of Product Liability*, Vol. 7, 1985.) $4.00.

Garber, S., *Product Liability and the Economics of Pharmaceuticals and Medical Devices*, R-4285-ICJ, 1993. $15.00.

Hensler, D. R., *Summary of Research Results on Product Liability*, P-7271-ICJ, 1986. (Statement submitted to the Committee on the Judiciary, United States Senate, October 1986.) $4.00.

_____ , *What We Know and Don't Know About Product Liability*, P-7775-ICJ, 1993. (Statement submitted to the Commerce Committee, United States Senate, September 1991.) $4.00.

Moller, E., *Trends in Civil Jury Verdicts Since 1985*, MR-694-ICJ, 1996. $15.00.

Peterson, M. A., *Civil Juries in the 1980s: Trends in Jury Trials and Verdicts in California and Cook County, Illinois*, R-3466-ICJ, 1987. $7.50.

Reuter, P., *The Economic Consequences of Expanded Corporate Liability: An Exploratory Study*, N-2807-ICJ, 1988. $7.50.

Punitive Damages

Carroll, S. J., *Punitive Damages in Financial Injury Jury Verdicts*, CT-143, June 1997. (Written statement delivered on June 24, 1997, to the Judiciary Committee of the United States Senate.) $5.00.

Garber, S., *Product Liability and the Economics of Pharmaceuticals and Medical Devices*, R-4285-ICJ, 1993. $15.00.

Hensler, D. R., and E. Moller, *Trends in Punitive Damages: Preliminary Data from Cook County, Illinois, and San Francisco, California*, DRU-1014-ICJ, 1995. Free.

Kakalik, J. S., P. A. Ebener, W. L. F. Felstiner, G. W. Haggstrom, and M. G. Shanley, *Variation in Asbestos Litigation Compensation and Expenses*, R-3132-ICJ, 1984. $7.50.

MacCoun, R. J., *Inside the Black Box: What Empirical Research Tells Us About Decisionmaking by Civil Juries*, RP-238, 1993. (Reprinted from Robert E. Litan, ed., *Verdict: Assessing the Civil Jury System*, The Brookings Institution, 1993.) Free.

Moller, E., *Trends in Civil Jury Verdicts Since 1985*, MR-694-ICJ, 1996. $15.00.

_____ , *Trends in Punitive Damages: Preliminary Data from California*, DRU-1059-ICJ, 1995. Free.

Moller, E., N. M. Pace, and S. J. Carroll, *Punitive Damages in Financial Injury Jury Verdicts*, MR-888-ICJ, 1997. $9.00.

_____ , *Punitive Damages in Financial Injury Jury Verdicts: Executive Summary*, MR-889-ICJ, 1997. $15.00.

Moller, E., E. S. Rolph, and P. Ebener, *Private Dispute Resolution in the Banking Industry*, MR-259-ICJ, 1993. $13.00.

Peterson, M. A., *Punitive Damages: Preliminary Empirical Findings*, N-2342-ICJ, 1985. $4.00.

Peterson, M. A., S. Sarma, and M. G. Shanley, *Punitive Damages: Empirical Findings*, R-3311-ICJ, 1987. $7.50.

Selvin, M., and L. Picus, *The Debate over Jury Performance: Observations from a Recent Asbestos Case*, R-3479-ICJ, 1987. $10.00.

Shubert, G. H., *Some Observations on the Need for Tort Reform*, P-7189-ICJ, 1986. (Testimony before the National Conference of State Legislatures, January 1986.) $4.00.

Mass Torts and Class Actions

Hensler, D. R., *Resolving Mass Toxic Torts: Myths and Realities*, P-7631-ICJ, 1990. (Reprinted from the *University of Illinois Law Review*, Vol. 1989, No. 1.) $4.00.

_____ , *Asbestos Litigation in the United States: A Brief Overview*, P-7776-ICJ, 1992. (Testimony before the Courts and Judicial Administration Subcommittee, United States House Judiciary Committee, October 1991.) $4.00.

_____ , *Assessing Claims Resolution Facilities: What We Need to Know*, RP-107, 1992. (Reprinted from *Law and Contemporary Problems*, Vol. 53, No. 4, Autumn 1990.) Free.

_____ , *Fashioning a National Resolution of Asbestos Personal Injury Litigation: A Reply to Professor Brickman*, RP-114, 1992. (Reprinted from *Cardozo Law Review*, Vol. 13, No. 6, April 1992.) Free.

_____ , *A Glass Half Full, a Glass Half Empty: The Use of Alternative Dispute Resolution in Mass Personal Injury Litigation*, RP-446, 1995. (Reprinted from *Texas Law Review*, Vol. 73, No. 7, June 1995.) Free.

Hensler, D. R., W. L. F. Felstiner, M. Selvin, and P. A. Ebener, *Asbestos in the Courts: The Challenge of Mass Toxic Torts*, R-3324-ICJ, 1985. $10.00.

Hensler, D. R., J. Gross, E. Moller, and N. Pace, *Preliminary Results of the RAND Study of Class Action Litigation*, DB-220-ICJ, 1997. $6.00.

Hensler, D. R., and M. A. Peterson, *Understanding Mass Personal Injury Litigation: A Socio-Legal Analysis*, RP-311, 1994. (Reprinted from *Brooklyn Law Review*, Vol. 59, No. 3, Fall 1993.) Free.

Kakalik, J. S., P. A. Ebener, W. L. F. Felstiner, G. W. Haggstrom, and M. G. Shanley, *Variation in Asbestos Litigation Compensation and Expenses*, R-3132-ICJ, 1984. $7.50.

Kakalik, J. S., P. A. Ebener, W. L. F. Felstiner, and M. G. Shanley, *Costs of Asbestos Litigation*, R-3042-ICJ, 1983. $4.00.

Peterson, M. A., *Giving Away Money: Comparative Comments on Claims Resolution Facilities*, RP-108, 1992. (Reprinted from *Law and Contemporary Problems*, Vol. 53, No. 4, Autumn 1990.) Free.

Peterson, M. A., and M. Selvin, *Resolution of Mass Torts: Toward a Framework for Evaluation of Aggregative Procedures*, N-2805-ICJ, 1988. $7.50.

_____ , *Mass Justice: The Limited and Unlimited Power of Courts*, RP-116, 1992. (Reprinted from *Law and Contemporary Problems*, Vol. 54, No. 3, Summer 1991.) Free.

Selvin, M., and L. Picus, *The Debate over Jury Performance: Observations from a Recent Asbestos Case*, R-3479-ICJ, 1987. $10.00.

Trends in the Tort Litigation System

Carroll, S. J., *Punitive Damages in Financial Injury Jury Verdicts*, CT-143, June 1997. (Written statement delivered on June 24, 1997, to the Judiciary Committee of the United States Senate.) $5.00.

Galanter, M., B. Garth, D. Hensler, and F. K. Zemans, *How to Improve Civil Justice Policy*, RP-282. (Reprinted from *Judicature*, Vol. 77, No. 4, January/February 1994.) Free.

Hensler, D. R., *Summary of Research Results on the Tort Liability System*, P-7210-ICJ, 1986. (Testimony before the Committee on Commerce, Science, and Transportation, United States Senate, February 1986.) $4.00.

_____ , *Trends in California Tort Liability Litigation*, P-7287-ICJ, 1987. (Testimony before the Select Committee on Insurance, California State Assembly, October 1987.) $4.00.

_____ , *Reading the Tort Litigation Tea Leaves: What's Going on in the Civil Liability System?* RP-226. (Reprinted from *The Justice System Journal*, Vol. 16, No. 2, 1993.) Free.

_____ , *A Glass Half Full, a Glass Half Empty: The Use of Alternative Dispute Resolution in Mass Personal Injury Litigation*, RP-446, 1995. (Reprinted from *Texas Law Review*, Vol. 73, No. 7, June 1995.) Free.

Hensler, D. R., and E. Moller, *Trends in Punitive Damages: Preliminary Data from Cook County, Illinois, and San Francisco, California*, DRU-1014-ICJ, 1995. Free.

Hensler, D. R., M. E. Vaiana, J. S. Kakalik, and M. A. Peterson, *Trends in Tort Litigation: The Story Behind the Statistics*, R-3583-ICJ, 1987. $4.00.

Moller, E., *Trends in Punitive Damages: Preliminary Data from California*, DRU-1059-ICJ, 1995. Free.

_____ , *Trends in Civil Jury Verdicts Since 1985*, MR-694-ICJ, 1996. $15.00.

Moller, E., N. M. Pace, and S. J. Carroll, *Punitive Damages in Financial Injury Jury Verdicts*, MR-888-ICJ, 1997. $9.00.

_____ , *Punitive Damages in Financial Injury Jury Verdicts: Executive Summary*, MR-889-ICJ, 1997. $15.00.

Peterson, M. A., *Summary of Research Results: Trends and Patterns in Civil Jury Verdicts*, P-7222-ICJ, 1986. (Testimony before the Subcommittee on Oversight, Committee on Ways and Means, United States House of Representatives, March 1986.) $4.00.

_____ , *Civil Juries in the 1980s: Trends in Jury Trials and Verdicts in California and Cook County, Illinois*, R-3466-ICJ, 1987. $7.50.

Peterson, M. A., and G. L. Priest, *The Civil Jury: Trends in Trials and Verdicts, Cook County, Illinois, 1960–1979*, R-2881-ICJ, 1982. $7.50.

Economic Effects of the Liability System

General

Carroll, S. J., A. Abrahamse, M. S. Marquis, and M. E. Vaiana, *Liability System Incentives to Consume Excess Medical Care*, DRU-1264-ICJ, 1995. Free.

Johnson, L. L., *Cost-Benefit Analysis and Voluntary Safety Standards for Consumer Products*, R-2882-ICJ, 1982. $7.50.

Reuter, P., *The Economic Consequences of Expanded Corporate Liability: An Exploratory Study*, N-2807-ICJ, 1988. $7.50.

Product Liability

Dunworth, T., *Product Liability and the Business Sector: Litigation Trends in Federal Courts*, R-3668-ICJ, 1988. $7.50.

Eads, G., and P. Reuter, *Designing Safer Products: Corporate Responses to Product Liability Law and Regulation*, R-3022-ICJ, 1983. $15.00.

_____ , *Designing Safer Products: Corporate Responses to Product Liability Law and Regulation*, P-7089-ICJ, 1985. (Reprinted from the *Journal of Product Liability*, Vol. 7, 1985.) $4.00.

Garber, S., *Product Liability and the Economics of Pharmaceuticals and Medical Devices*, R-4285-ICJ, 1993. $15.00.

Hensler, D. R., *Summary of Research Results on Product Liability*, P-7271-ICJ, 1986. (Statement submitted to the Committee on the Judiciary, United States Senate, October 1986.) $4.00.

_____ , *What We Know and Don't Know About Product Liability*, P-7775-ICJ, 1993. (Statement submitted to the Commerce Committee, United States Senate, September 1991.) $4.00.

Peterson, M. A., *Civil Juries in the 1980s: Trends in Jury Trials and Verdicts in California and Cook County, Illinois*, R-3466-ICJ, 1987. $7.50.

Punitive Damages

Carroll, S. J., *Punitive Damages in Financial Injury Jury Verdicts*, CT-143, June 1997. (Written statement delivered on June 24, 1997, to the Judiciary Committee of the United States Senate.) $5.00.

Garber, S., *Product Liability and the Economics of Pharmaceuticals and Medical Devices*, R-4285-ICJ, 1993. $15.00.

Hensler, D. R., and E. Moller, *Trends in Punitive Damages: Preliminary Data from Cook County, Illinois, and San Francisco, California*, DRU-1014-ICJ, 1995. Free.

Kakalik, J. S., P. A. Ebener, W. L. F. Felstiner, G. W. Haggstrom, and M. G. Shanley, *Variation in Asbestos Litigation Compensation and Expenses*, R-3132-ICJ, 1984. $7.50.

MacCoun, R. J., *Inside the Black Box: What Empirical Research Tells Us About Decisionmaking by Civil Juries*, RP-238, 1993. (Reprinted from Robert E. Litan, ed., *Verdict: Assessing the Civil Jury System*, The Brookings Institution, 1993.) Free.

Moller, E., *Trends in Civil Jury Verdicts Since 1985,* MR-694-ICJ, 1996. $15.00.

_____ , *Trends in Punitive Damages: Preliminary Data from California,* DRU-1059-ICJ, 1995. Free.

Moller, E., N. M. Pace, and S. J. Carroll, *Punitive Damages in Financial Injury Jury Verdicts,* MR-888-ICJ, 1997. $9.00.

_____ , *Punitive Damages in Financial Injury Jury Verdicts: Executive Summary,* MR-889-ICJ, 1997. $15.00.

Moller, E., E. S. Rolph, and P. Ebener, *Private Dispute Resolution in the Banking Industry,* MR-259-ICJ, 1993. $13.00.

Peterson, M. A., *Punitive Damages: Preliminary Empirical Findings,* N-2342-ICJ, 1985. $4.00.

Peterson, M. A., S. Sarma, and M. G. Shanley, *Punitive Damages: Empirical Findings,* R-3311-ICJ, 1987. $7.50.

Selvin, M., and L. Picus, *The Debate over Jury Performance: Observations from a Recent Asbestos Case,* R-3479-ICJ, 1987. $10.00.

Shubert, G. H., *Some Observations on the Need for Tort Reform,* P-7189-ICJ, 1986. (Testimony before the National Conference of State Legislatures, January 1986.) $4.00.

Law and the Changing American Workplace

Darling-Hammond, L., and T. J. Kniesner, *The Law and Economics of Workers' Compensation,* R-2716-ICJ, 1980. $7.50.

Dertouzos, J. N., E. Holland, and P. A. Ebener, *The Legal and Economic Consequences of Wrongful Termination,* R-3602-ICJ, 1988. $7.50.

Dertouzos, J. N., and L. A. Karoly, *Labor-Market Responses to Employer Liability,* R-3989-ICJ, 1992. $7.50.

Peterson, Mark A., Robert T. Reville, and Rachel Kaganoff Stern, with Peter Barth, *Compensating Permanent Workplace Injuries: A Study of the California System,* MR-920-ICJ, 1997. $20.00.

Stern, Rachel Kaganoff, Mark A. Peterson, Robert T. Reville, and Mary Vaiana, *Findings and Recommendations on California's Permanent Partial Disability System: Executive Summary,* MR-919-ICJ, 1997. $8.00.

Victor, R. B., *Workers' Compensation and Workplace Safety: The Nature of Employer Financial Incentives,* R-2979-ICJ, 1982. $7.50.

Victor, R. B., L. R. Cohen, and C. E. Phelps, *Workers' Compensation and Workplace Safety: Some Lessons from Economic Theory,* R-2918-ICJ, 1982. $7.50.

Compensation Systems

System Design

Darling-Hammond, L., and T. J. Kniesner, *The Law and Economics of Workers' Compensation,* R-2716-ICJ, 1980. $7.50.

Hammitt, J. K., R. L. Houchens, S. S. Polin, and J. E. Rolph, *Automobile Accident Compensation: Volume IV, State Rules*, R-3053-ICJ, 1985. $7.50.

Hammitt, J. K., and J. E. Rolph, *Limiting Liability for Automobile Accidents: Are No-Fault Tort Thresholds Effective?* N-2418-ICJ, 1985. $4.00.

Hensler, D. R., *Resolving Mass Toxic Torts: Myths and Realities*, P-7631-ICJ, 1990. (Reprinted from the *University of Illinois Law Review*, Vol. 1989, No. 1, 1989.) $4.00.

_____ , *Assessing Claims Resolution Facilities: What We Need to Know*, RP-107, 1992. (Reprinted from *Law and Contemporary Problems*, Vol. 53, No. 4, Autumn 1990.) Free.

King, E. M., and J. P. Smith, *Computing Economic Loss in Cases of Wrongful Death*, R-3549-ICJ, 1988. $10.00.

Peterson, Mark A., Robert T. Reville, and Rachel Kaganoff Stern, with Peter Barth, *Compensating Permanent Workplace Injuries: A Study of the California System*, MR-920-ICJ, 1997. $20.00.

Peterson, M. A., and M. Selvin, *Resolution of Mass Torts: Toward a Framework for Evaluation of Aggregative Procedures*, N-2805-ICJ, 1988. $7.50.

Rolph, E. S., *Framing the Compensation Inquiry*, RP-115, 1992. (Reprinted from the *Cardozo Law Review*, Vol. 13, No. 6, April 1992.) Free.

Stern, Rachel Kaganoff, Mark A. Peterson, Robert T. Reville, and Mary Vaiana, *Findings and Recommendations on California's Permanent Partial Disability System: Executive Summary*, MR-919-ICJ, 1997. $8.00.

Victor, R. B., *Workers' Compensation and Workplace Safety: The Nature of Employer Financial Incentives*, R-2979-ICJ, 1982. $7.50.

Victor, R. B., L. R. Cohen, and C. E. Phelps, *Workers' Compensation and Workplace Safety: Some Lessons from Economic Theory*, R-2918-ICJ, 1982. $7.50.

Performance

Abrahamse, A., and S. J. Carroll, *The Effects of a Choice Auto Insurance Plan on Insurance Costs*, MR-540-ICJ, 1995. $13.00.

Carroll, S. J., and A. Abrahamse, *The Effects of a Proposed No-Fault Plan on the Costs of Auto Insurance in California: An Updated Analysis*, IP-146-1, January 1996. Free.

Carroll, S. J., and J. S. Kakalik, *No-Fault Approaches to Compensating Auto Accident Victims*, RP-229, 1993. (Reprinted from *The Journal of Risk and Insurance*, Vol. 60, No. 2, 1993.) Free.

Carroll, S. J., A. Abrahamse, and M. E. Vaiana, *The Costs of Excess Medical Claims for Automobile Personal Injuries*, DB-139-ICJ, 1995. $6.00.

Carroll, S. J., A. Abrahamse, M. S. Marquis, and M. E. Vaiana, *Liability System Incentives to Consume Excess Medical Care*, DRU-1264-ICJ, 1995. Free.

Carroll, S. J., J. S. Kakalik, N. M. Pace, and J. L. Adams, *No-Fault Approaches to Compensating People Injured in Automobile Accidents*, R-4019-ICJ, 1991. $20.00.

Carroll, S. J., and J. S. Kakalik, with D. Adamson, *No-Fault Automobile Insurance: A Policy Perspective*, R-4019/1-ICJ, 1991. $4.00.

Hensler, D. R., M. S. Marquis, A. Abrahamse, S. H. Berry, P. A. Ebener, E. G. Lewis, E. A. Lind, R. J. MacCoun, W. G. Manning, J. A. Rogowski, and M. E. Vaiana, *Compensation for Accidental Injuries in the United States*, R-3999-HHS/ICJ, 1991. $20.00.

_____ , *Compensation for Accidental Injuries in the United States: Executive Summary*, R-3999/1-HHS/ICJ, 1991. $4.00.

_____ , *Compensation for Accidental Injuries: Research Design and Methods*, N-3230-HHS/ICJ, 1991. $15.00.

King, E. M., and J. P. Smith, *Economic Loss and Compensation in Aviation Accidents*, R-3551-ICJ, 1988. $10.00.

O'Connell, J., S. J. Carroll, M. Horowitz, and A. Abrahamse, *Consumer Choice in the Auto Insurance Market*, RP-254, 1994. (Reprinted from the *Maryland Law Review*, Vol. 52, 1993.) Free.

O'Connell, J., S. J. Carroll, M. Horowitz, A. Abrahamse, and D. Kaiser, *The Costs of Consumer Choice for Auto Insurance in States Without No-Fault Insurance*, RP-442, 1995. (Reprinted from *Maryland Law Review*, Vol. 54, No. 2, 1995.) Free.

Peterson, M. A., *Giving Away Money: Comparative Comments on Claims Resolution Facilities*, RP-108, 1992. (Reprinted from *Law and Contemporary Problems*, Vol. 53, No. 4, Autumn 1990.) Free.

Peterson, M. A., and M. Selvin, *Mass Justice: The Limited and Unlimited Power of Courts*, RP-116, 1992. (Reprinted from *Law and Contemporary Problems*, Vol. 54, No. 3, Summer 1991.) Free.

Rolph, J. E., with J. K. Hammitt, R. L. Houchens, and S. S. Polin, *Automobile Accident Compensation: Volume I, Who Pays How Much How Soon?* R-3050-ICJ, 1985. $4.00.

Special Studies

Hensler, D. R., and M. E. Reddy, *California Lawyers View the Future: A Report to the Commission on the Future of the Legal Profession and the State Bar*, MR-528-ICJ, 1994. $13.00.

Merz, J. F., and N. M. Pace, *Trends in Patent Litigation: The Apparent Influence of Strengthened Patents Attributable to the Court of Appeals for the Federal Circuit*, RP-426, 1995. (Reprinted from *Journal of the Patent and Trademark Office Society*, Vol. 76, No. 8, August 1994.) Free.

An annotated bibliography, CP-253 (12/97), provides a list of RAND publications in the civil justice area through 1997. To request the bibliography or to obtain more information about the Institute for Civil Justice, please write the Institute at this address: The Institute for Civil Justice, RAND, 1700 Main Street, P.O. Box 2138, Santa Monica, California 90407-2138, or call (310) 393-0411, x6916.